To

_____

From

St. John's Lutheran Church
Bellevue, Ohio   June 1989

"The Lord will keep
your going out and your coming in
from this time forth and for evermore."

Psalm 121:8

Today and Tomorrow

ALVIN N. ROGNESS

AUGSBURG Publishing House
Minneapolis, Minnesota

TODAY AND TOMORROW

Copyright © 1978 Augsburg Publishing House

Library of Congress Catalog Card No. 77-84095
International Standard Book No. 0-8066-1621-0

Design and photos: Koechel Design; page 8, John Thornberg

Scripture quotations unless otherwise noted are from the Revised Standard Version of the
Bible, copyright 1946, 1952, and 1971 by the Division of Christian Education of the National
Council of Churches.

MANUFACTURED IN THE UNITED STATES OF AMERICA

To Nora
mother of six
Michael
Paul
Stephen
Martha
Peter
Andrew

Contents

Today and Tomorrow

Life is not bits and pieces. It's a road, from birth to death—and beyond death.

It has bends and curves. It dips into valleys. It plunges into chasms. It climbs into soaring mountains. It stretches through plateaus of fragrant woodlands. It crosses arid deserts.

It's the road we travel, from yesterday through today and into the tomorrows.

High school years are full of people and events. No other part of the road will yield such frustrations and fears, such exuberance and hope.

It's a good road, but there are many turns. Perhaps the sharpest turn of all comes with the end of high school. Then comes college or a job and leaving home. Overnight boys and girls are reclassified as men and women.

But the road rolls on with rich promise.

Yesterday was good, today is good, tomorrow will always promise more.

Stop the clock!

Today is a good day. Tonight is graduation, and I was just over at the school to turn in some sheets of music. I have a feeling that I love everyone in school—my class, my teachers, the janitors, even the walls. I'd like to stop the clock so today would never end.

You will have many other good days, but none exactly like this one. High school graduation is a high point. If you find a good job or go on to college and even earn a doctor's degree, no day will top this one.

I have known people who bypass their college class reunions, but they cross continents to have a day with their high school teachers and friends. You will do that too. You may not even write to them, but 10 or 15 years later when the class reunion invitation arrives, you will feel the strong pull to get back to the old school and the old friends.

God has a way of letting us forget the times we were fed up with school, with teachers, and even with friends. Instead, we remember the good things. It's happening to you already. And there have been far more good times than bad.

You are saying something today that I hope you can say every day of your life. You are saying, "Today is good." You will have days filled with sadness and disappointments, but you will never have a day without hidden blessings, if you look around for them.

Each day has a way of gathering together the memories of our yesterdays and our dreams for the tomorrows. That's why the *now* is so rich.

We chop up time into years and months and days and hours. But time is more like a flowing stream, or perhaps like a winding road with many curves and bends.

The sharpest bend, I think, is the end of high school. You will soon leave home. Our society regards you as an adult. If you get into trouble, you are no longer ushered into juvenile court. Society says, "Now you're on your own." This bend in the road is an abrupt one.

Don't be afraid of it. Throughout high school you have gradually been making more and more decisions on your own. Once away from home, you won't have your parents to meddle or to lean on. But don't forget that they will still be on the road with you, with their prayers and their love, and with their help when you want it.

The world is waiting for you. It's not a big, bad world. It's a big, good world. God created it, and "God saw that it was good." An evil force invaded it, but evil could not overcome goodness. Out there in the world, all kinds of people and all sorts of situations are waiting for you to give them your best.

Tomorrow is an exciting stretch of road.

Why be afraid?

From up on the platform with the rest of the class, I could see the whole town. My parents, my brother and sister, my uncles and aunts were all there. It was fun looking at them. I think they were proud. They told me the speaker was good, but I hardly heard him. My mind got to wandering. I started thinking about what the next years would be like, and I was scared.

Four years ago you didn't know whether you would ever finish high school. Now you have your diploma, and that's good. If you think of life as a race, you have now finished one lap, and you are already running the next one. Who knows? It may be a better one than the last.

Probably all of us are scared as we look into the future. No one can know what tomorrow will be like. Adam and Eve must have been frightened as they left the garden. And how about Moses, as he left Midian to face Pharaoh in Egypt? And Abraham Lincoln, when he thought of what the nation would be like after that terrible Civil War?

Fear is natural to everyone. Of course you don't know what the next years will be like. No one does. Tomorrow may bring good news or bad news.

You would have to be asleep or just plain stupid if you didn't have some fear. But you don't have to let fear paralyze you.

Fear has nothing to do with whether you have courage. A young paratrooper during World War II said he never did get over being scared as he jumped out of the plane. The 20th jump was as bad as the first. He said, "I was always frightened, but I never hesitated. When it was time to jump, I jumped, and it was always a thrill to have the ropes tighten and to feel myself floating through the air."

Take a look at the fears you have felt. How many of the bad things you thought might happen actually did happen? You wasted a lot of nervous energy over nothing, didn't you? Remember that.

Haven't you discovered that some things you thought were bad luck actually turned out to be good luck? You were afraid it would happen, and it did. But it turned out differently from how you had imagined.

Let's say you apply for admission to the college of your choice and are turned down, so reluctantly you go to another. But there you meet the one who becomes your partner in marriage. It seemed like bad news to be turned down, but it really was good news.

You will sometimes meet people who have a dismal view of the future. Everything looks dark. They have given up on life itself. Nothing adds up to anything. Do you remember this bleak picture in Shakespeare's *Macbeth?*

Tomorrow, and tomorrow, and tomorrow creeps in this petty pace from day to day to the last syllable of recorded time, and all our yesterdays have lighted fools the way to dusty death. Out, out, brief candle! Life's but a walking shadow, a poor player that struts and frets his hour upon the stage and then is heard no more. It is a tale told by an idiot, full of sound and fury, signifying nothing (V, v).

Some people today take this blighted view. They think of nuclear arms, world hunger, unemployment, pollution, exhaustion of energy supplies— and they are ready to give up on any future for anyone.

Norman Cousins, editor of *Saturday Review,* told one college graduating class, "No one knows enough to be a pessimist." I like that. You don't have to be a pessimist. You have a lot of things going for you. You made it through high school—and that's very important.

The world holds many bad things, but it also offers plenty of good things. Think of a few accomplishments in this century alone. We have airplanes, radio, television, computers. We've routed many of the old killers—smallpox, diphtheria, pneumonia, polio. Think what the next 50 years may uncover for your good and for the world's good.

The world needs you. Somewhere it has the right place for you. If you don't drop out in fear or discouragement, but day by day do what lies handy to do, doors will open.

Best of all, God has a place for you. He is around to see that things don't fall apart. And he has given each of us a good formula. He tells us not to be overanxious about tomorrow, but to do today what needs to be done.

When he teaches us to pray, "Give us this day our daily bread," he is telling us not to put in our order for 10 years or 50 years, but for a day at a time.

You would have to say that yesterday was a good day. You graduated from high school. And how about all the other yesterdays? There were some good ones, right?

Do you remember the line from the hymn "Lead, Kindly Light"? "So long thy power hath blessed me, sure it still will lead me on."

Leaving parents

Sometimes I've looked forward to leaving home and not having my parents looking over my shoulder all the time. They worry too much. It's almost as if they don't trust me. And they act as if they own me. Still, I know I'll miss them. But I want to leave. I don't want to hang around home any longer.

Sure, they worry. Good parents always do. You will worry too if you have a family of your own. They worry because they care.

Let me tell you a little secret about parents. They want to be needed. When you were a baby, you needed them for everything. This was a great time for them. They may have grown tired of wiping your nose and washing your diapers, but there was no question about being needed.

Gradually, you needed them less and less. You did things for yourself and on your own. Your high school years may have been difficult for them, because you may have decided that you could get along fairly well without them and their ideas. You'd let them pay for your clothes and see that you had a car when you needed one, but you could get along without their advice. That was hard on them. They wanted you to need their advice too.

17

Did you ever hear about the 16-year-old who thought his parents were behind the times, and who, coming home at 22, was amazed to see how much they had learned in six years?

Your parents will always have a great stake in you. That's the price they pay for having you as their child and loving you. You will be the source of some of their greatest joys, and maybe their greatest hurts.

But they can't drop you. God has put us together into families, and we can't escape. Now that you are leaving home, let your parents feel that they are still needed, and not only for their money.

Keep in touch with them. Write. Phone. They won't mind if you call collect. Remember, they're still worrying about you. They won't be lying awake, checking on when you come in at night or asking whether you have your assignment done. They will worry, not because they trust you so little, but because they know that the world you face is not always a pleasant place.

In their prayers, when they thank God for the good things in their lives, you will be on top of the list. And when you pray, you will thank God that he gave you these particular parents.

In their letters to you, they may not push you about faith, prayer, and church, but you can be sure they will be delighted to have you share your experience in prayer. They will appreciate hearing about your connections with a church, and that you've met some good friends there.

As the years go on, you will be more and more in their thoughts. Their minds will be running off to you more than when you were underfoot. As they rattle around in the house without you, they will probably make albums of your pictures, wait for your letters, report about you to the neighbors, and count the days until your next visit.

The years will do something like that for you too. The irksome things about your high school days at home will fade, and you will remember the good times. God is gracious to help us forget the bad and remember the good.

If you marry some day, they will be wise enough to relax their hold on you. They will know that in a very special way you now belong to someone else, to your marriage partner and to your children if you have any. But they will enlarge their hearts to include those who have become dear to you.

Until they die, that's the way it is, thank God!

Why compete?

Finally—I made it! I remember saying to myself when I was a freshman that I'd be valedictorian of my class. I worked hard for grades and got them. With my 97.5 average I was .2 ahead of Jim. And I don't think he even thought much of grades or of being at the top. My parents were proud, especially Mother. Now that graduation is over, I have a let-down feeling.

Why should you feel let down about reaching your goal? It must be satisfying to be the best student in the class.

I'm not even sure that I am the best student, or that I have the best mind. I suppose I was the best competitor. I wanted to be at the top more than anyone else.

Is there anything wrong with that?

> Maybe not wrong, exactly. But I keep comparing myself with Jim. I don't think he ever thought that he was competing for grades with me or with anyone else. He just seemed to enjoy doing his work well and he didn't worry about grades.

But I thought Jim was one of the best athletes in school. He surely was a competitor there, wasn't he?

> Yes and no. I don't think even then he cared much for himself. He didn't worry about whether he or someone else ran the most yards, as long as the team scored touchdowns. And in the 440 or the half-mile, he was running against the clock and to make points for the school. I don't think he worried about being best in anything.

But why should you feel that being best doesn't make any difference?

> I'm not sure I understand either. I'm glad I'm valedictorian, but I'm beginning to think there's something wrong with always wanting to be at the top. It's not just in school. If you're always working to be better than someone else—smarter, richer, more powerful—maybe you stop caring what happens to other people. Isn't that true? Maybe it even makes you feel good when other people fail.

Yes, I think I see that danger. But you must have the satisfaction of knowing that you are intelligent, that you have a good mind, and that you will be able to cope with life.

> I'm not even sure of that. There are different kinds of intelligence. I remember things well, like in history and literature. But I had a dreadful time with geometry. Some kids who mostly got Cs in history got easy As in geometry. And other kids didn't get very good grades in anything, but I know they're smart in things that don't involve books. They'll probably end up as top salesmen or executives.

I think you're selling yourself short. To be an A student is certainly proof that God has given you a good mind. Besides, you've had to use discipline and determination. Those are good qualities.

Yes, I know. But I shouldn't have wanted so much to be better than anyone else. I should have wanted to do the job well, without worrying if someone had done it better. I think Jim was genuinely pleased that I beat him and got what I wanted. I couldn't have been pleased if he'd been valedictorian. Don't you see that by competing against others, and by wanting to win for my own satisfaction, I was blocking myself out from enjoying anyone else's winning?

I guess that's right.

Besides, the kids knew that I was gunning for first place, and that stood them off. I never had the easy-going friendships in school that Jim had.

I guess I'm glad for Mom's sake. She wanted to be top student in her class 25 years ago, and didn't make it. Now, in a way, she's made it through me. But it's still wrong.

She said, "I'll bet you can be valedictorian in college too." But whether I win top honors in college or not, I intend to enjoy studies and friends in college more than I did in high school. I've learned that I don't need to be first to be good—or to be satisfied!

A job's a job

The job I have is terrible. I'm already sick of it. I stand on the assembly line and every 28 seconds I pick up a refrigerator panel and hang it on a passing hook. Eight hours a day! That's about a thousand panels each day. I'm counting the days until summer is over and I can go to school or find another job.

It doesn't sound too interesting, I agree. But some people work assembly lines the year around, and they have to come to terms with their jobs. Years ago, you may have assembled a whole refrigerator by yourself. That kind of work might be more interesting, but if that were how we got our refrigerators, a lot of people would go without.

Do a little arithmetic. There are 168 hours in a week, and you have only 40 hours on the line. You have 128 hours left. You'll have to sleep some, say 50 hours. That leaves 78 hours to fill with all sorts of interesting things. It wasn't many years ago that people in factories worked 10 or 12 hours a day and at least six, sometimes seven days a week.

Don't feel sorry for yourself. You have a job. That's something. Some of your friends can't find work at all.

23

I'm glad you're looking forward to something else, college or a more demanding job. But for the moment let's consider people who do the same thing over and over, day after day, year after year. How can such people find fulfillment? How can they think of themselves as doing a service for others?

Let's assume a man is on an assembly line. He tightens one bolt on the wheel of a car as the frame passes by. Is that important? Suppose he is careless and doesn't fasten the wheel securely. You buy the car, and one day on the freeway the strain is too great and the wheel spins off. You swerve across the highway into speeding traffic and are killed. The man on the assembly line is responsible.

But if that man is good and conscientious, he knows he has your life in his hands, almost as surely as if he were a surgeon removing a brain tumor. If he has imagination, he might be thinking of the thousands of lives he may have saved by tightening that one bolt just right.

But he's not just the man who tightens that bolt. He is a husband and a father. He belongs to a church and sings in the choir. He's on a bowling team with friends. He reads books and likes music. He belongs to his labor union. He is a citizen, and he votes in elections.

Fortunately, life is more than work. Even an executive of a big corporation had better learn that simple but basic lesson.

All work is important enough to be done well. Luther once said that a maid could sweep the floor to the glory of God as surely as a pastor could preach a sermon to the glory of God. And not because she sings a hymn while she sweeps. God likes clean floors—it's as simple as that. All work is honorable if it is done well. Of course, that would hardly hold true if your occupation were robbing banks!

It will probably be several years before you settle on the kind of work you will be doing until you're 70. You may have many jobs on the way. If you go to college, you may change your major interest more than once.

I like what a friend of mine, now president of a major college, once said: "I've liked every job I've had, from delivering papers to driving a truck to teaching. I like what I'm doing now too." Guiding a big college is not an easy job, and he may sometimes wish he were back driving a truck, but I'm sure he would never admit it.

Work is not punishment. Thank God you have a job.

Finding friends

Soon I'll be leaving most of my good friends. Will I be able to get along without them? Will I find others? That's what worries me. If I go to college or get a job somewhere, is there any chance that I can have friends like the ones I've had in high school?

They may not be standing around the corner waiting for you, but they are out there somewhere. You will find them, or they will find you.

Don't be too eager to become pals with anyone who comes along. As you well know, friendship is no casual thing. If someone you hardly know says, "Friend, we've got a beer bust going tonight" or "Why not join us for a little pot?" you can be fairly sure that this would be a poor start for friendship. You don't have to be rude, but you can be selective.

If you go to college, especially if the college isn't large, you should have no trouble learning to know many people. Some of them will become your fast friends.

If you take a job in a new town or city, you may have to plan a little strategy. You will find some friends on the job. But you will want to look in other places. The best place may be the church. If you don't know anyone, introduce yourself to the pastor and he will help you widen your circle. People may at first look a bit stiff and even cold, compared with those in a singles bar. But if you're open to it you will find lots of friendship waiting.

Whether in a bar or in a church, you may be going about finding friends the wrong way. You can't collect friends the way you gather pebbles on the beach.

Jesus gives a clue. He said, be a friend. Look around for people who need you as a friend, not for people you might use as friends.

Once when Jesus told people to love their neighbors (friends) as themselves, a lawyer interrupted him to ask, "And who is my neighbor?" In answering him, Jesus told the story of the good Samaritan.

A man had been mugged and lay unconscious in the ditch. This man from Samaria came along, picked up the stranger, took him to the inn, left some money, and promised to pay the whole bill. Finishing the story, Jesus turned the question around and asked the lawyer, "Who proved neighbor (friend) to the man?"

The big question is not how many friends you can find, but how many people you can find who need you as a friend.

Jesus doesn't say whether the Samaritan ever got to know even the name of this stranger. He may have left the inn before he returned to pay the bill. But imagine what a wonderful man this Samaritan was, going around caring for people who needed a friend. He wasn't concerned whether they paid him back in friendship or not. You may say, "But he must finally have had a lot of friends, even if he never tried to collect them." I'm sure you're right.

The reason you have had good friends in high school is no doubt because you have been a friend. Keep on being a friend, and don't worry about how many friends you can collect. There are all sorts of people, some lonely, some discouraged, who need you as a friend. Find them.

A good teacher

Some teachers I've had were good and some were not so good. Mr. Froiland was the best. I'll always remember him. We really learned math from him. But that wasn't all. He liked kids and you knew it. He gave you the impression that you, and not math, were the most important. If I could be as good a teacher as Mr. Froiland, I'd be a teacher.

You are lucky to have had Mr. Froiland. You learned math, and that's important. More than that, you learned that people are important. You probably could learn math from a computer or a correspondence course, but you couldn't learn love except through another human being.

One of the reasons there aren't more Mr. Froilands is probably that students themselves make it hard for teachers to love them. It takes a lot of love for a teacher to care about students if they are rude and inattentive.

If you are headed for teaching as your life's work, you are picking one of the most important roles. Along with being a parent (and parents are certainly teachers for their children), teaching is central in the life of society. You will deal with ideas, and ideas grow wings and carry a person into life. If the ideas are wrong, life will be wrong. As Proverbs says, as a man "thinketh in his heart, so is he" (Prov. 23:7 KJV).

As a teacher, you set the direction for the lives of the people you teach. Even if the direction is right, a person needs skills and knowledge to reach a goal. So you'll have to work hard to master your field, whether that be math, history, languages, or whatever. You wouldn't have thought as much of Mr. Froiland, even though he was thoughtful, if he had known nothing about math. He was both a first-rate teacher and a caring human being.

You will be going into college now, if you plan to be a teacher. Give it all you've got. Get everything you can from your teachers, from the library, and from every course. Whether you'll be an A or B or even C student won't matter as much as if you work up to your capacity. Many C students have become excellent teachers.

Looking back on your high school years, you may be sorry that you neglected some of your courses. You will have to make it up in college. Why pay tuition if you don't collect the dividends?

When at 17 I first hired out on a farm for the summer, my father (who had a general store in a small town) gave me three rules: Do everything Mr. Johnson tells you to do. Then ask him if there's anything more he has for you to do. If he says no, then look around for something to do on your own.

You might try that in college. Don't settle for only the work your teachers assign. Look beyond the assignments. Have the intellectual curiosity to develop interests of your own.

We live in a wonderful country where practically everyone who wants to can get a college education. In many lands, only a select few receive an advanced education. And what you will pay in tuition is but a fraction of the cost of your schooling. Through taxes and through generous gifts, the people of this land have made it possible for you to be as educated as you want to be.

College years can be great years. Give them your best.

Smart hands

Working with my hands—that's what I like best. And I don't mean writing essays or doing bookkeeping. I love motors, carpentering, anything like that. My parents are glad that I'm handy, but I think they want me to be a lawyer or a business executive. I doubt that I'll go to college at all. Maybe some vocational school, but not college.

Parents are like that. If one father says, "My son is going to law school," the other father may hesitate to say, "My son isn't going to college, he's going to be a plumber," even though a plumber may make more money than the lawyer.

My mother and father had only grade school educations. Both were anxious that their five sons and one daughter finish college. We did finish. One became a certified public accountant, one a teacher of piano and organ, two college teachers, and two pastors. I think my parents were more pleased than if one of us had become a carpenter and contractor, even if it would have meant earning far more money. My parents' generation (and mine too) had the notion that a person who sits behind a desk, has clean fingernails, and reads books has "made it."

31

This is changing, in part because people with Ph.D.s are having trouble getting jobs. Some drive cabs. Some work in filling stations. We have no trouble finding teachers, but where can you get a good electrician?

A surgeon can get you through a health crisis. But there are other kinds of crises. Your lights go off, your refrigerator doesn't work, your car stalls —now what? You need someone with skills. The surgeon can't do anything for you. The teacher of philosophy has nothing from Plato to help. The professor of theology can't help you from the Bible. But if you are an electrician or mechanic, you can bring relief. You have skills in your hands to help.

People who work with their hands have brains too, and they use them. Their brains are not in neutral just because they have skills in their hands. There are many kinds of intelligence. They are not all geared to reading books and working at desks.

If you choose an occupation that doesn't require a B.A. degree, you can be as enlightened a citizen, as fine a parent, as good a neighbor, and as effective a member of a congregation as any professional person, and you may even read as many books.

Don't ever be ashamed of choosing an occupation for which you work mostly with your hands. The important thing is to do well whatever you decide to do. If carpenters always cut corners, the things they built wouldn't last. You will be responsible to the people who buy your services.

A man may be a fine plumber who would have been a poor teacher. A woman might have been happy as a forester, but she's miserable as a lawyer. Or she's absorbed in art, but would have found nursing a drudgery.

I'm glad there are people who like to work with their hands. You may be just the person I need.

Little things

Why do I let little things bother me? I know I shouldn't, but I do. If the teacher praises someone else's paper and not mine, I get moody. If my parents have the car and I'm waiting to use it, I sit around and stew. I wonder how I'd take big troubles, if small ones throw me.

You would probably surprise yourself. If you were in an accident and hospitalized for several months and had to give up school for a term, you might take it in stride. People are more often done in by small irritations and disappointments, or a piling up of them, than by big troubles.

When my father's store burned to the ground one dry October night, I wondered if he would go to pieces. I had seen him often irritated by small adversities. To my surprise, he didn't even lose his cheerfulness. He got a smaller building and was in business another 25 years.

It's a pity that we let little things get us down, when we can meet big crises well.

Our joys come from little things too, more than from big things. Kind words from someone you love bring more happiness than a new car. A new car is a used car after a hundred miles. If you understand this, you can find thousands of opportunities to make people happy.

33

I think it was Napoleon who said, "Men are governed by trifles." A boy applied as a page in a bank, only to be told that the position had just been filled. Sad, he turned to go. On the way out, he stooped to pick up a pin that someone had carelessly dropped. As he replaced it on the desk, the president said, "I think we can use you." Thirty years later the boy was president of the bank.

You may remember the little ditty about the cavalry soldier:

For want of a nail the shoe was lost;
for want of a shoe the horse was lost;
for want of a horse the rider was lost;
for want of a rider the battle was lost—
all for the want of a two-penny nail.

Your high school diploma is the outcome of hundreds of small assignments you took seriously. You have friends because in many small ways you showed that you cared about them. Your life is the sum of small things.

On the other hand, we all have to learn not to be thrown for a loss by trifles that should be shrugged off or forgiven or cushioned by a sense of humor. Suppose your father in a moment of exasperation says, "How stupid can you be?" You'd be silly to conclude that your father is finally admitting his disdain for you, or to brood about being so stupid that you'll never amount to anything. Far better if you say to yourself, "Dad must have had a hard day at the office" or "His arthritis is getting to him."

Knowing how inclined we all are to be influenced by small things, you can set out on a career of helping people with little courtesies and small tokens of concern.

It was only a glad "Good morning,"
As she passed along the way,
But it spread the morning's glory
Over the livelong day.
CHARLOTTE AUGUSTA PERRY

You greet someone, you thank someone, you send a letter or you telephone someone, and the day is a bit brighter with cheer and courage.

Of all people who ever lived, Jesus was most sensitive to the needs of people. And of course he met the biggest need of all the earth—he died for the sins of the world.

But in the three years that he walked around Palestine, he was always noticing small, ordinary people, cheering them and comforting them. He keeps on doing this today. The moment you turn to him, to your surprise you will discover that he was there all the while, waiting. Small needs and big ones are all the same to him.

In joining him, you will be able to put small things in their proper place. The small irritations that threaten to "get" you, you can virtually dismiss—with forgiveness and humor.

And you can turn the little things of life into occasions of warmth and cheer to the many people who are longing for just that.

One family

Now I'm going to church again, but it's not my denomination, and my folks don't like it too well. A new friend of mine invited me to her church, and I really like it. I don't see why my parents should care as long as I go to some church that has the same Bible and the same Lord.

They may not be as troubled as you think. Each of us who has grown up in one denomination may have only vague impressions of the many churches that make up the large Christian family. So it's perfectly natural that everyone, including your parents, feels most comfortable with the familiar.

Almost every Sunday all Christian churches confess that we believe in the holy Christian church. You and your parents realize that your own denomination is but a part of something much larger to which you belong.

Suppose you think of the church as one army, with one flag and one leader. The army may be broken up into many regiments. Each regiment will have its own history, its own flag, perhaps its own songs. The soldiers in each regiment may boast that theirs is the best regiment in the army.

There's nothing wrong with that, unless the regiments get the notion that they are not in the same army, and that they have to fight each other. This, sad to say, has happened in the army of the Lord.

The Baptists, the Episcopalians, the Methodists, the Catholics, the Lutherans, the Congregationalists, and others, are regiments. They have but one leader, the Lord Jesus Christ, and they have but one book of common instructions, the Bible.

In their separate histories, they have developed differences. But the churches are one. There's no way for them not to be one, because they have the same leader.

People don't often shift from one regiment, or denomination, to another. They have the Lord and the Scriptures in their own church, so why change? On the other hand, we can benefit from learning how people worship in another church. And occasionally there could be good reasons for shifting.

It's rarely good to shift because you've gotten fed up with your own church. Every congregation may have its rough periods, and then some people will leave, but it's precisely then that they ought to stay and help.

I gather that you're not unhappy with your own church, but for the time being you've found it good to be in this one. You're finding a warmth of concern and caring in this group, and that's good. It may be just what you need now, and it doesn't have to mean that you'll be leaving your parents' regiment.

All Christian churches of the world need to discover that they are one family. Most of them have not bothered to know much about other churches. They have often behaved as if they were strangers, and even rivals or competitors.

We can be much encouraged with what's been happening during this century. Beginning with a great Missionary Conference in Edinburgh in 1910, with the formation of the World Council of Churches in 1948 and Vatican II of the Catholic church in 1962, the churches that have Jesus Christ as Lord have drawn together as never before. We are discovering that we are one family.

And that's exciting. It's almost like going back to the days of the disciples and the early centuries of the church. The followers of Jesus had one simple confession, "Jesus is Lord," and all who worshiped him were one fellowship. With all the denominations we have today, we are still one fellowship, across national and racial borders.

We even cross the borders of death. Those who have died in the Lord are now what we call "the church triumphant." Their battle against evil and for the Lord is ended, and they've gone on to enjoy the victory the Lord has won for them.

It's a great company—the church on earth and the church in heaven. In whatever regiment, be glad you're one of them.

Having children

Probably I'll get married sometime, but I'm not going to have any children. I don't think it's right to bring someone into a world with so much danger as ours. Who knows what terrible things they may have to face? Nuclear war, pollution, maybe even starvation.

I had friends 50 years ago who said they wouldn't be guilty of bringing children into this kind of world. Admiral Nelson of the English fleet said it in his day. And it's never been said more eloquently than in the Book of Ecclesiastes (and that's about 3000 years ago):

> I have seen everything that is done under the sun; and behold, all is vanity and a striving after wind. So I hated life. And I thought the dead who are already dead more fortunate than the living who are still alive; but better than both is he who has not yet been, and has not seen the evil deeds that are done under the sun.

I understand how you feel. I have 12 grandchildren, and when I read a newspaper or watch TV I wonder, with some fear, what their world will be like before they reach my age. Under no condition, however, could I wish that their parents had decided not to give me any grandchildren.

Nor am I sure how noble or how moral your resolution is. If every person in your generation should be as "moral" as you, the human race would end before another century is over. Is that what you think best?

Could it be that we are losing both courage and hope? We give up on the world. We think of catastrophic things that might happen to take away the comforts and conveniences of our technological civilization, and don't feel up to coping. Our pioneer grandparents who fought the blizzards, drought, grasshoppers, and prairie fires were tough, but we have grown soft. Could it be?

More likely, you have grown cautious because of what's happening to families in our day. You see children who are victims of broken homes. You see diminished support for the values and disciplines necessary for fulfillment. You read of children brutalized by harassed parents. You see young people, even from good families, caught up with drugs and disillusionment. So you conclude that you will be kind enough not to usher anyone into this spreading jungle.

But if you are sensitive to the storms that threaten, for that very reason you may be most eligible to take on the responsibility of a family. There will be children, whether you bring them into the world or not. And others may be less qualified to care for them, and for the world, than you are.

It will take courage—more courage than for my generation, I am convinced. But there may be a little girl or boy standing in the wings, waiting for you to give them a chance to take the stage, a girl or boy who would give beauty to your life and to the world, and who, despite the pains that they may have to endure, would be eternally grateful that you didn't let them stay waiting (nonexistent) in the wings forever.

Healed memories

How do you handle bad memories? I don't have many, but there are a few I'd like to get rid of. It scares me when I read that we store in our subconscious everything that we've ever done or experienced. I've done some things I'm ashamed of, and if they're festering in my brain, I'd like to get at them.

Psychologists may overplay the subconscious, but sometimes I have dreams that dredge up out of the past the craziest combination of things. So I suppose it's all there, somewhere.

You talk about memories festering in your brain like a sore festering in your leg. If that's a valid comparison (and I think it is), then memories need healing.

I know very little about strategies psychologists and psychiatrists use. I know they can be very helpful. They are most helpful when they recognize that we need God as a healer. We all remember things we've done wrong. No one but God can handle those memories.

We remember events that generated great fear or panic, perhaps a terrible storm or an accident. Somehow, the fear digs itself into our subconscious. The crisis is over, but the fear is still hiding and may cause trouble.

41

A young man who lived through an earthquake as a boy never got over the panic of that moment. The fear dug itself into his brain, and by the time he was 19 he had to quit school. He was in and out of hospitals. Doctors tried to help, but the fear remained.

Then he came into the hands of a devout woman who "prayed" the fear out of him. She put him into the hands of God, whose love simply drives out fear. Call it "divine healing" or whatever. It worked. He still had the memory of the earthquake, but the paralyzing fear that followed was gone. He was nestled back into the everlasting arms. He was healed.

But what about getting rid of bad memories you have created? Did you cheat? Did you lie? Did you deceive your parents? Did you play around with the gift of sex? Did you take a run at shoplifting?

These memories can be crippling. They can rob you of joy. They can even make you look into the future with less than hope. And try as you will to push them aside and say, "Well, everyone does it, and it isn't that important," you know that's not true. Some people think they can push it all down so far into forgetfulness that it won't bother any more. But memories fester.

There is but one way of healing for wretched memories. *Jesus forgives sins.* He not only forgives. He promises to forget all about them. Once forgiven, they are gone, "as far as the east is from the west."

Jesus died on a cross precisely to take away the sins of the world, including yours. All the failures and wrongs of your life can be swept out of your subconscious, out from you utterly, and deposited with him. He takes them, removes them, and forgets them. And he orders you to forget them too.

If you have wronged someone specifically, you may want that person's forgiveness too. If you have hurt someone, and can do something for healing, this you may need to do.

But at the very heart of life, with God himself, the memories are all taken care of. He has destroyed them, and he commands you to let them go too.

You will have a harder time forgetting than God. But you not only have a right to forget, you have a duty to forget. God does not want your mind (conscious or subconscious) cluttered with paralyzing memories that will keep you from a full and rich life. He wants you equipped to serve him. And you can't drag these memories around if you are going to do a glad job for him.

You are still young. You have most of life ahead of you. Try as you will to keep from other failures, you will accumulate more wretched memories.

Don't forget what to do with them. Your Lord is waiting to take away your guilt, your fears, your festering memories. And he is glad every time you place them in his hands.

Everybody's book

They tell me that the Bible is still the best seller. I'm puzzled. Few people seem to read it. Even in Sunday school we had other books. In our home it lies on the end table day after day. I've read parts of it, but I have trouble with the Old Testament, where God seems to command the killing of men, women, and children. How can we think of the Old Testament God as the same God we meet in Jesus?

Don't say that you haven't read the Bible. Your Sunday school books were all taken from the Bible. Every church service is full of the Bible. The pastor preaches from the Bible. Most hymns are indirectly from the Bible.

You're right. Not many people read the Bible, at least not regularly and not from cover to cover. Perhaps we should. With serious study, it can be a most engrossing book.

We all have problems understanding it. But start with Jesus. He is not hard to understand. And he isn't vengeful, like some pictures of God in the Old Testament. Remember that the Israelites may have been mistaken when they thought God ordered them to kill. Not until Jesus did God reveal himself fully. That's why the Christian church believes that the Old Testament by itself is an incomplete picture of God. The God of the New Testament is the clear picture.

Of all the books in the world, the influence of the Bible is without rival. It has shaped civilizations. We must remember that for more than 1300 years, until Gutenberg (1397-1468) and the movable press, the Bible was read only by scholars who could read Greek, Hebrew, and Latin. Since then, printing presses have turned out Bibles at tremendous speed. At least one book of the Bible has been translated into more than 1500 languages and dialects.

The Bible is like no other book. That's why it keeps selling. The Bible is God's Word to the world. God is in the book. If you read it for information (like you read any other book), you risk getting more than information. You risk meeting God and being captured by him.

And unlike all other books of religion about gods and goddesses, the Bible pictures a God of great love. Even the Old Testament, in spite of the puzzling image you get from wars, has amazing accounts of God's mercy. Read Psalm 23 and Isaiah 53, 54, 55, for instance.

In Jesus (God the Son) we know what God is like and what he has done for us. He became one of us to die for us. In some wonderful way beyond our understanding, that was God's way of expressing his love for us. Anyone faced with this tremendous truth can never be the same again.

Give yourself a chance to love this book. Read it. Don't be satisfied with reading about it, or reading books inspired by it.

When you find parts that speak especially to you, memorize some of them. Say them over to yourself again and again. They will become like inner pillars of your soul. You will rest your life on them.

What should I be?

I might have known he'd ask. Uncle Charlie is like that. He's a doer. He likes to brag a little—how he started with nothing and became a success. I guess he's loaded. He came to my graduation, and he asked, "Well, my boy, what are you going to do with your life?" I didn't have an answer, at least not the kind of answer that would have sounded OK to Uncle Charlie. The fact is, I don't know. I wish I did, but I don't.

Uncle Charlie and others like him have built this country. They have been enterprising, they have worked hard, they've had single-minded ambition. It may be hard for them to understand why every young person would not be geared up to go places.

On the other hand, it is not strange that young people may not yet be sure what they want to do. It may take several years before you are settled on a profession or vocation.

You've probably had vocational tests or guidance in high school that show your aptitudes. These tests are helpful, but they can't be conclusive. If the tests show that you are good in math, and if you like math, someone may have advised you to become an engineer or an accountant.

47

That formula isn't good enough. If you were good at robbing banks, and you liked to rob banks, that wouldn't mean that you had a calling to rob banks.

I know a young man who had a straight A average in college math and physics, and who had a full scholarship for a doctoral degree at Massachusetts Institute of Technology. But as a senior in college, he felt a call to become a pastor. No vocational test would have told him to enter the ministry. But he did, because he was convinced that he could serve the world better by preaching the gospel.

Ask yourself how, with your ability, can you best serve God, other human beings, and the world. This could lead you into any number of occupations —law, farming, engineering, medicine, business, teaching. There are many honorable occupations, and in any of them you can be of service.

Don't let money be the test. If you do your work well in any of the standard occupations, you'll have enough money. It would be a mistake if you became a lawyer for the fees instead of to help people achieve justice, or if you chose medicine because in our country most doctors become wealthy.

Whatever skills you achieve should belong to the people who need the service of those skills. They may be able to pay you a reasonable fee, but that must not be the reason you give service to them. Suppose you were a scientist and you discovered a sure cure for cancer. If you wouldn't cure anyone until they had paid you $1 billion, wouldn't the world have a right to be enraged? You would owe the world the cure, simply because millions of people in the world need it.

Uncle Charlie and others of his generation were hard workers. They didn't have their eyes on the clock. Your grandparents' generation was even more industrious, attacking the vast prairies with ax and plow. But with machines, electricity, and the computer, we now talk about a three-day workweek—three days of work, four days of no work, and retire at 62. Every year we have more new sophisticated machines to be our slaves and spare us work.

Your generation will have to come to terms with leisure time. What will you do with it? More pointless trips on the highway? More hours before the tube?

Some of you will be Charlies all over again. You will moonlight several jobs. You will throw yourselves into work that will make you richer and richer.

Some of you will decide this rat race is not for you, and you will drop out altogether or drift from one thing to another.

You don't have to do either. You don't have to wear yourself out in the race for money or prestige, and you don't have to drift. The extra time that you have can be channeled into a hundred ways to make life better for your family and your community. This will take imagination, more imagination by far than your grandparents needed attacking the land.

Even more than imagination, it may demand a fresh look at what life is all about. Jesus didn't say much about work. He warned repeatedly against accumulating material things. He said a good deal about caring for one another.

If you take Jesus seriously, there will be no end to what can be done with extra time. He told us that whatever we did for people in need we would be doing for him.

Whenever life can be turned around so it isn't a mad chase for security, money, property, power, or pleasure—a new day dawns. Perhaps it's up to you and your friends to show this old world—all of us Uncle Charlies— a new day.

Is life fair?

Compared with the Rockefellers, our family isn't rich. But compared with most people I know, we've really made it. We have three cars and a swimming pool. We run off on expensive vacations. Mom and Dad give away some of their money, but they sure aren't hurting. This doesn't seem right to me.

We might wish that everyone in the world had the same amount of money and possessions, but there have always been rich and poor. This is not to say that God likes it that way or that he has set out to make some rich and others poor.

Jesus recognized this unhappy gap, but did not suggest an economic order that would take from the rich and give to the poor. Robin Hood did that. Instead, Jesus laid down a clear rule for the use of money. He said, "Every one to whom much is given, of him will much be required." He never intended those who had money to keep piling it up. He intended that they use it in service of him and of people in need.

How we get money is as important as how we use it. If a person becomes wealthy by making unfair profits or by charging excessive fees and commissions, even if it is legal, it's wrong. It's virtually stealing from the consumer or patient or client.

Lack of fairness is not only a private problem. It's a national and international one. Year by year the gap widens between people who have much and people who have little. In the United States, for instance, if the total wealth were $32, one person would have $8, 49 people would have 50¢ each, and 50 people would have 2¢ each. And Americans, with 6% of the world's population, have 40% of the world's wealth.

You and your generation may be able to correct these inequities. If you end up with more money than you need, you have a double task—first, to be generous with your gifts, and second, to carefully consider whether your profession or business should not correct its system of profits and fees. Eventually, if this is not done voluntarily by people who care for fair play, the government must step in to fix fees and profits. This is never as satisfactory as if it is done voluntarily.

Don't wait until you become rich (if you do) before you begin to do the right thing with money. Even when you can well use it yourself, start giving some of it away. The Bible suggests 10% for the work of the Lord. And cut back on what you need or think you need. The uncomfortable fact is that the American economy depends on people buying all sorts of unnecessary products and services. Advertising keeps assuring us that we need and deserve things when in most cases we simply don't.

In the long run Americans and even the growing industrial Third World cannot continue consuming the world's resources at the current rate without simply running out of minerals, energy, and food. So don't feel that you're betraying your country or the world's future if you cut back from the standard of living that your parents' generation has.

You may feel helpless to do anything about many aspects of this problem. But you can do something about yourself. You can play the game by the right rules, whatever others may do.

First, be honest and fair about how you get money. There's a delightful story about a man who bought a farm and accidentally dug up a box with thousands of dollars in bills. He returned the box to the former owner, who

51

said, "No, it's not mine, because I didn't even know it was there." But the buyer insisted, "No, it's yours. I bought the farm, not this box of money." I don't remember how they settled the matter, but wouldn't it be wonderful if everyone tried to be as honest and fair as that?

Then, again, learn how to give. And start early. You will learn the truth of the Lord's words, "It is more blessed to give than to receive."

Running away

Maybe you've got the answer. How come we hear so much about the danger of smoking tobacco and so little about the danger of drinking alcohol? And why do some parents get upset if their kids smoke marijuana and just laugh if they get drunk?

I don't have the answer. Early in this century America had a constitutional amendment against the possession and use of any form of alcohol, even beer, but no one then gave a second thought to smoking tobacco.

Now the pendulum has swung to the other extreme. In 1933 we repealed the amendment prohibiting alcohol, and since then the sale of alcohol has been wide open, except to minors. Meanwhile, we've had a national scare about tobacco contributing to cancer and heart disease. Very little is said about the much greater danger of alcohol to the heart, liver, and brain.

Alcohol is a drug, the most widely used of all drugs, and the most easily obtained. There are obviously other drugs that cause more immediate and more lasting damage, but none compares in scope of damage with alcohol. How many highway deaths, how many broken homes, how many lost jobs, how many early graves are the result of alcohol?

Why do people drink? Initially alcohol is a stimulant, and a modest amount in a mixed drink or beer or wine "lifts the spirits," relaxes a person, and adds a little zest to the conversation. But if you don't stop there, it becomes an escape from life, a device for running away.

A British captain stationed in Calcutta years ago was drinking heavily in the bar one night. His friend took him by the arm and said, "You've had enough." The captain lifted his glass, drained it in a gulp, and said, "My friend, this is the swiftest passage out of India."

Your generation has experimented with a variety of other drugs, often with disastrous results. I don't know why you do. Are you running away too? And from what?

Anyone who has used these drugs knows that in running away from failure, unpleasant people, or general disgust with the world, you're running, not uphill to sunlit meadow, but downhill to a cave filled with monsters.

If you have friends who are already trapped in the cave, you can help by getting them into the hands of professionals ready to give them a lift back to the light. Among other things, back to the light means back to God.

A person who has given up needs friends, needs help from trained people, and needs a higher power—God.

Sometimes we all feel like escaping and forgetting. We start running, and all doors seem closed—except alcohol and drugs.

But there is always another door. Jesus said, "I am the door."

Playing God

Last week we had a frightful scare. Jane tried to commit suicide. She took a whole bottle of sleeping pills, washed them down with Coke, and went to bed to die. Her mother found her. They brought her to the hospital in time and flushed out her stomach. She was unconscious for two days. We all wonder why she would do a thing like that. Grandpa says that if she had died, she would have gone to hell.

God, and not your grandpa, is the judge. And he is a God of infinite mercy.

Why did she do it? Who knows? Only God can tell. It would be folly for people to judge, to place blame: "Her parents had let her down." "Her teachers were too hard on her." "Her boy friend wasn't nice to her."

It is cruel to try to play God. If you want to be an analyst, ask what you might have done for Jane that you failed to do. Don't look to others.

We are all fragile. Our hearts beat because God keeps them beating. Some day they will stop. Our brains function with reason because God keeps them functioning. Some day they may start slipping cogs. Jane's may have slipped a cog or two.

The death of any young, promising person—whether by automobile accident, cancer, war, or suicide—is sad. The death is the tragedy, not the manner of death. For loved ones, grief over death is enough to bear without grieving over the manner of death.

Psychologists tell us that everyone probably has a death wish at one time or another. Sometimes we get ourselves into a corner, the future looks dark, and we may think, "If I died, I wouldn't have to worry about it." Rarely does the wish grow strong enough so we do anything rash. But occasionally things get so dark that someone slips over the precipice.

The right to choose one's own death has always been thought wrong. God said, "Thou shall not kill." In recent times the question has surfaced, especially for older people and people with a fatal disease, "Do I have a right to ask that my life be ended?" Your generation will have to deal with this tormenting question.

I'm glad Jane didn't die. She will be glad too. I remember being called to the bedside of another girl who tried to kill herself. She had become so discouraged that she gave up on the future. Later she finished college and married a good man, and they have three fine children.

Don't add to Jane's sense of guilt by treating her differently from before—except, perhaps, to be sure that you become a real friend.

She found Jesus

I've lost my best friend. She joined some kind of strange religious outfit. They have a tight little group down in a warehouse that they've fixed up. She tells me that now at last she has found Jesus and is following him. I thought we all believed in Jesus in Sunday school and church and were trying to follow him. She says we are all wrong. She even thinks her parents are wrong. And if there are any nicer people than her folks, I'd like to know who they'd be.

I doubt that you have really lost her. She'll be back. For a moment she has taken a detour in her religious life. This is a time for you to be patient with her. After all, she thinks that she has found something very important. Maybe she has.

There have always been groups spinning off from the church. Back in the early centuries, the Desert Fathers left the cities and the regular church life and formed little cells in the desert. These were devout men who dedicated their lives to prayer. Most famous was Simeon Stylites, who lived on top of a pillar for many years.

A few years ago I visited a Trappist monastery near Dubuque, Iowa. Trappist monks take a vow of silence. They are not allowed to speak to one another, only to God. Eleven hours a day they give to prayer. Our guide said, "These men are making up for all the prayers you do not pray."

Some groups today are not Christian spinoffs. They don't regard Jesus as Lord and Savior. Many of these movements are phony, hardly religious, organized for the profit of their leaders.

But apparently the little group your friend has joined is something different. She has found Jesus in the center of her faith. And that is good. What is not good is that she has begun judging what is truly Christian and what is not, turning her back on you and on her family. Only God can know the heart, and she thinks she can know. In one sense, she has pushed God out of the throne and sits on it herself. I'm sure God is not happy with that!

Most groups like this have certain emphases that are not good. I can think of four. First, they are off by themselves away from the larger family of churches. Second, most of them believe the world is so bad that nothing can be done to make it better. Third, they think scriptural prophecies tell them that the Lord is about to come again in glory (the Lord himself said that no one can predict this), and all they have to do is to sit by and wait for that day. And fourth, many of them have leaders who use people for their own prestige, or for money.

In all fairness to her, perhaps we ought to ask what made your friend join this group. Did she find most people in her church not following Jesus as the Bible teaches? Maybe she saw them take up all sorts of things that seemed to ignore Jesus. They went to church when they felt like it, they bought expensive homes and cars, they dashed off on costly vacations. To be sure, they gave money to the church, but not sacrificially. Maybe she began to wonder, "Is this what Jesus asks of us?"

We may look too much like the ancient church in Laodicea, to which the Lord addresses himself in Revelation 3:15-17:

57

> I know your works: you are neither hot nor cold. Would that you were cold or hot! So, because you are lukewarm, and neither cold nor hot, I will spew you out of my mouth. For you say, I am rich, I have prospered, and I need nothing; not knowing that you are wretched, pitiable, blind, and naked.

Maybe we're just easygoing Christians, and your friend has reacted against the style of religion she sees in us. But she shouldn't give up on the church. By her own more serious attempt to be a follower, she should show the rest of us what dedication we lack. She probably hopes to do that by leaving, but she shouldn't have to leave to influence us.

She may think that all followers of Jesus will have, or should have, the same experience she has had. She forgets that God has made us all different and that he apparently likes variety in his family. Now she has isolated herself in a small group that no doubt feels exactly as she does. That takes her away from the larger and richer mixture of God's children.

Try to keep in touch with her. But don't hope that she will give up on this fresh loyalty to Jesus and drift back to being a lukewarm follower.

Let's be honest with her and with ourselves. We are a rich country. We have large homes and good cars. We buy boats and snowmobiles. We run off on vacations to Hawaii and Europe. Even we who don't take expensive trips have more of everything than we need. How do you become a faithful follower of Jesus in this affluent world?

Simeon Stylites retreated to the desert, the Trappists to their monastery, and your friend to her group. But that is not the best answer, certainly not for most of us. In the thick of this fast-moving world, we must find ways to use our resources and our time to help people in need, to make the world a better place.

Be patient. Your friend has withdrawn into her little group, but she'll come back to a world that needs her. She won't stay in the desert or the monastery forever.

Sex is special

*T*his business of sex gets to me. I don't know what to think. We don't talk about it much in my home, but I know my parents are old-fashioned. They think you should wait until you're married. Most parents are like that, I guess. But some of the kids don't care what their parents think. They say times have changed. They don't think any more about having sex after a date than I do of kissing a girl goodnight.

Times haven't changed since Noah, at least not on this subject. These kids haven't found a new freedom. They are only drifting into a practice that has tempted people in every age. And it's a practice that gives a moment's pleasure at the risk of much later unhappiness.

The sex act belongs to marriage, between one husband and one wife. It does not belong between friends, and it does not belong between a couple who just find each other attractive. Sex is too special for any relationship outside marriage, where two people love each other deeply and have promised to care for each other for a lifetime.

Sex is a way you give yourself to another as part of a larger package of love. Sex is not a way you use someone for pleasure. Some day you will

59

find someone you love, someone you would like to care for until you die. Perhaps you have already found that someone. If she gets crippled, OK. If he becomes blind, OK. If she has moments of depression, OK. You love that "someone." You give yourself. You want to make your mate happy. And that's where sex belongs. Sex is a part of giving yourself to each other.

God understands us better than we understand ourselves. After all, he put us together. He knew what he was doing when he laid down rules against fornication (sex between two unmarried persons) and against adultery (sex between married people outside their own marriage). These rules are for our protection, and to help us find the kind of happiness that doesn't grow sour.

If some older man would be frank with you, he would tell you God's rules make sense. If the man ever played around with sex, he'll tell you he wishes he hadn't. If he waited and lived with a woman for a lifetime, he will tell you that nothing could be better.

Others may be drifting, but don't join them. Others are buying in on those momentary pleasures, but don't buy. You will never be sorry. When the right person comes around and you marry, you will be ready for a lifetime of joy.

Am I being used?

This summer I worked in a restaurant. About the third night I waited on a guy I really liked. He liked me too. We've been going together all summer now. Last night he really upset me. He asked me to live with him in his apartment. What should I do? I have the most scary feeling. I'm not sure what I'd be getting into. But if I say no, will I lose him? Will he find someone else for his apartment? I really like him.

I'd like to ask you some questions. Do you mind?

> Not if they would help me.

First let me say that yours isn't exactly a new problem. Men have had mistresses (sometimes called concubines) from ancient times. They simply used someone to sleep with. Rarely would they marry them. Kings and nobles did this brazenly. Everybody knew it. And occasionally a queen or princess would latch on to some young man for sex. If she got tired of one she would get another. Do you think your situation is like that?

> I sure don't. We love each other. If I thought it would be like that, I'd give him up this minute.

Are you sure? Aren't you only hoping that he isn't just going to use you for a year or so? And are you certain that as you get to know each other in bed, he'll want to marry you?

> Of course. That's what he said. He thinks of this as a kind of marriage, and so do I.

Doesn't it bother you that he hasn't asked you to marry him?

> Well, yes. Whenever I've thought of actually living with a man and going to bed with him, I thought it would be my husband. If I live with him now, I'd like to think of this as a marriage in fact, even if it isn't public. I don't think that's a sin, do you?

Let's think about that. It isn't the marriage license from the courthouse that makes a marriage. The promise that each makes to the other, to live together "till death us do part," is the heart of the marriage. Are you promising each other that you will live together and love each other until you die?

> We haven't gone that far yet. If I do live with him, that's what I hope would happen.

If it doesn't, then what?

> I suppose we'd quit living together.

Then what?

> I don't know. That bothers me. I've always dreamed of loving someone and caring for him a lifetime. I'd hate to think of sharing one apartment after another with different men all my life. That would be terrible.

If you do live with him now, would you tell your parents?

I'd hate to tell them. I'd hope they wouldn't need to know.

Why?

They would be terribly hurt. They have such high hopes for me, and I wouldn't want to disappoint them. They would never understand. And I suppose they would hate Bob, although I'm sure they would like him as my husband.

If he's that good, why do you suppose he doesn't want to marry you right now and have it all in the clear? The marriage license, the church service, the celebration, and the whole bit?

I'm not sure. I guess it's because he believes the license and the church service are not what makes a marriage. He's talked about people who have a service with all the trimmings, and then after a few years they divorce. Maybe he doesn't want to make promises like that.

I can understand that a person shouldn't make promises and then break them. But do you think that's a good reason for not making any promises? Isn't it possible that the reason Bob doesn't want to make promises in public is that he really doesn't think of living with you for a lifetime? After all, you know of people who live together for a few months and then it's over. Maybe that's what he has in mind.

If I thought he did, I wouldn't go for it. He's really a wonderful guy and I love him. I don't want to lose him.

What if you told him you love him enough to marry him, but not enough to be his wife in a secret hole somewhere? If he really loves you, don't you think he'd love you all the more because you want him for a lifetime? If he's decent he wouldn't want to hurt your parents, or his parents either. He certainly wouldn't want to hurt you.

Maybe.

It could be that deep down he is thinking, "When I get married for keeps, I want the kind of girl who wouldn't shack up with anyone, not even with me." Men are funny that way.

But I doubt that he's ready to get married. He wants to go to law school, and I have four years of college ahead. How could we get married now?

You could. People have. And your parents (and his too) would rather you married if you're going to live together. If you don't think you're ready for marriage, it might be better to wait, even if you lose him. If your love for each other is real, it will last. If it's not, one way to kill it altogether is to pretend secretly that you're married when you're not.

But haven't people grown to love each other more in bed?

Yes. A lot of married people can tell you that's true. But they have had the open support of the people around them, the church, the family, friends. You would have none of that. Besides, you would have an uneasy conscience to deal with, which doesn't do much for love.

You make it sound pretty impossible.

Not altogether. Some couples who started this way have made it into a deeper love and a good lifetime marriage. But the odds are against you. There are big risks. It could turn out to be one of the saddest things you have ever done.

What if I say yes, and the whole thing goes sour in a few months? What do you think would happen to me?

I think you would be deeply hurt. But I hope you would remember that God forgives every wrong, every failure. Like a bird with a wounded wing, you may never fly as high and as far as you might have, but you will fly God's grace will carry you on.

A good land

During our course on government we got a grand idea of what our country is like. Then I read in the newspapers about senators and representatives having affairs with women and cheating on their income tax, and I get depressed. Is it true, like some books say, that our kind of government is on the rocks, and that we finally will go to tyrants and military dictatorships?

Don't worry too much about the newspapers. We have a great, free press. But for the most part, the papers print the bad news about a few leaders, and not the good news about the great majority of leaders. And there are many trying to do the best, most honest job they know how to do.

Of course, any democracy has to count on honest leadership. If we didn't have that, we would be in deep trouble. We are a government of law, and if our leaders consistently ignored or violated the law, we couldn't survive as a free people.

But do we have a right to ask our leaders to be more honest than we are? If people in general cheat on their income tax, pad their expense accounts, cheat on school examinations, do a little shoplifting, falsify

65

applications for jobs, steal each others' husbands and wives, and don't bother to study the issues of government—can we expect such people, elected to office, suddenly to turn around and be honorable? As the people go, so goes the country.

Long ago, Plato said democracies could not survive because people were too lazy to study the problems of self-government, and, if they did, they were too selfish to support legislation for the common good. In an especially pessimistic note, an American humorist said that only 5% of the people think, another 10% think they think, and the other 85% would rather die than think.

That's a dark picture but you don't need to buy it. Our democracy has survived for 200 years. People and leaders have defied the laws, to be sure, but they rarely got by with it. Leaders who break the law are seldom reelected.

I'd like to say three things to you.

First, I hope you will resolve to be the kind of citizen any community would be proud to claim. This means being honest. It means being willing to study the issues and to support every good cause, even if there's nothing in it for you. It means having courage and hope. It means living by those God-pleasing values that alone can bless a nation.

Second, perhaps you should have an eye on some political office. Why shouldn't you think of taking your turn on the school board, as mayor of your town, in your state legislature or even in the national Congress?

Third, be careful that you do not become cynical about your country. This land has a long history of devoted and able leaders. And ask yourself what other countries have such freedoms as we enjoy. We should be grateful and proud.

The risk of love

How much does a person dare to love? If you give too much of yourself, aren't you going to get hurt? I've seen girls crushed when some guy dropped them. I have a friend whose mother died, and he just wasn't himself for months. Maybe it's safest never to care too much.

You are so right. It is safest. The risks of love are great. If you love someone, you give him a whip. He can hurt you. If your chief concern in life is not to get hurt, don't love anyone.

Go ahead, use people, and don't get attached to them. Then when you no longer need them or when you tire of them, you can drop them and go your way. You don't get hurt. They may, but so what? That's their lookout.

In the days of slavery, black people were property. They were bought and sold like horses, usually cheaper than horses. Many owners did get attached to them, but there were many others who would grieve more over losing their favorite riding horse than over the death of a slave.

The days of slavery are over, but we are still tempted to use people. Industries use people for work and call them simply "labor supply." A man and woman use each other for sex, and dismiss it as a passing affair. If they can manage to stay detached, maybe they won't get hurt.

69

But deep down every person wants to be loved and wants to love. Try as you will, you can't avoid the risks, hurts, and scars—and (if you play the game right) the deep joys of love.

And the rules of the game are not hard to understand. Treat every person as someone very important. Remember that every person can be easily hurt. Set out to bring joy, and not hurt, into the lives of people you touch. You won't succeed 100%. There is only one who ever did, and he lived almost 2000 years ago. But your life will be richer because you've tried.

Death is once

Once in a while I get to thinking about death—not often, but when I do it's no fun. I don't want my parents to die, or my brother. And I don't want to die. I'd like to live to have a husband and children, and become a grandmother. Is everyone afraid of death? Does God decide on a time for each person to die?

I think all of us are afraid, some more, some less. Perhaps people who have lived a long time have no fear of death, especially if they are ill and in much pain and if they have faith, so they can look forward to something much better. But there is no rehearsal for death. It's a one-time event, and I think everyone is uneasy about it.

Fortunately, God has given us a strong instinct for life. Even when things look dark and we have great disappointments, we still want to live.

No, I don't think God has an appointed time for each person. The psalmist says, "The years of our life are threescore and ten," 70 years. But this hardly means that God wants everyone to live precisely that long, no more and no less.

From the Bible it seems that God planned for us to live forever, and that death is an intruder. Death is here in opposition to God. It's as if God says to death, "So you did get in, you scoundrel. I will let you have your little time with my child, but the minute you are through with her and can't do any more, I will put her on her feet again in another, more wonderful part of my empire. She will live there forever with me, and you can't touch her anymore."

Jesus, who died to forgive our sins and give us back to the Father, gave this beautiful promise to his followers:

Let not your hearts be troubled; believe in God, believe also in me. In my Father's house are many rooms; if it were not so, would I have told you that I go to prepare a place for you? And when I go and prepare a place for you, I will come again and will take you to myself, that where I am you may be also (John 14:1-3).

Even with this great promise, most of us want to live here on God's good earth as long as we can. There is work to do here, and there are things to enjoy here. God has put us here, and we are in no hurry to have death come. Nor is God in a hurry to receive us on the other side.

Our second son, Paul, was killed instantly in an accident as he was on his way home from two years at Oxford University in England. At age 24, everything looked bright for him. Then in a twinkling he was dead.

I recalled at the time some words from Robert Ingersoll's funeral sermon for his brother who had died as a young man: ·

> He died where manhood's morning almost touches noon, and while the shadows still were falling toward the west. He had not passed on life's highway the stone that marks the highest point. . . . And yet it may be best, just in the happiest, sunniest hour of all the voyage, while eager winds are kissing every sail, to dash against the unseen rock, and in an instant hear the billows roar above a sunken ship.

We were not able to think of it as best for Paul, or for us. His life had been full, to be sure, with friends he loved and who loved him. But we all thought it was too soon.

But we can't measure the excellence of a painting by the size of the canvas or the excellence of a life by its length. And none of us knows how big our canvas on earth will be. On the other side we will have an endless one.

As long as we live on earth, each day we are adding a touch to the picture we will leave for those who come after us. Whether the canvas is big or little, the years short or long, the picture is the thing!

I hope you will worry very little about how many years you will have or how many your parents will have. May you and they have many, and may you paint on your canvas beautiful things—the love of friends, of a mate and children, even grandchildren.

Hidden glory

All my life I've thought of myself as a religious person. I believe in God. But when Jesus says, "You shall love the Lord your God with all your heart, and with all your soul, and with all your mind," I'm puzzled. How can you love someone you've never seen or touched or heard? I love people, like my mother, but I can see her, I can feel her arms when she hugs me, I can hear her voice call, "Time to get up!" Could I love her if she had died when I was born and I'd never have seen her? How can I love God?

You can, and you do. But it's a miracle.

God hides behind masks. He helps us to love the masks. More than that, he prods us to keep trying to look behind the masks to get at him. And he has promised that if we look for him, we will find him.

The masks are something like windows covered with thin frost. Through the windows you see outlines, the shape of a tree or a man, but you can't distinguish features.

Let me tell you about three masks God uses.

73

The first is his Word and sacraments, his church. But, you say, that's not God. That's right, but God is lurking in everything that's there.

From the time you were a baby, you probably have been within the world of the church. You learned to lisp some prayers, to sing songs about God. As you grew, you memorized certain parts of his Word, the Lord's Prayer, Psalm 23, John 3:16.

Far more than you know, the church and all it stands for has gotten into your bones. It's part of you. You may have drifted from it now and then, but it has a deeper place in your heart than you think. There are hymns, for instance, that will stir something within you till you die:

> Jesus loves me, this I know, for the Bible tells me so. . . .
> I love to tell the story of Jesus and his love. . . .
> Praise God from whom all blessings flow. . . .
> The Church's one foundation is Jesus Christ her Lord. . . .

If someone tells you, "Sure, you have an attachment to the church, but that's not God," don't be disturbed. God is glad that you have a love for his mask, because this is a way of loving him.

Another of his masks is the universe itself. The psalmist sings, "The heavens are telling the glory of God; and the firmament proclaims his handiwork. . . ."

The far reaches of the sky, the blazing sunset, the myriad of stars, the flowers, the trees that stretch their arms toward heaven—all this is a window through which your imagination (or your faith) sees God and loves him.

It's a pity if all you see in the wheeling galaxies is the marvel of mathematics or the precision of a machine. Behind it all is God, who made it all and called it good. When the Russian astronauts returned to earth and reported that they saw nothing of God out there in space, they were saying nothing about God. They were only admitting that they had no window.

The third mask is people, good people and bad people, smart people and dull people, rich people and people in need. They all bear the likeness of God, who created them in his image. God wants them all eventually to live with him forever. No one is a run-of-the-mill person, a cousin of the chimpanzee. We all have the stamp of God on us.

And God comes into view especially through people who have learned to love. Your mother's love for you is a reflection of God's love for you. Many people fail to reflect this love, and all of us fail some of the time. But whenever love breaks through the self-centered crust, you glimpse outlines of the shape of God.

Also, God appears in needy people. In *The Vision of Sir Launfal,* a young knight sets out in search of the Holy Grail, the cup Jesus used at the last supper. As he leaves on his horse, the sight of a beggar at the gate fills his heart with disgust. Much later, after years of futile search, he returns to his castle. At the gate is the same beggar. Suddenly Sir Launfal's heart surges with love for him. Then a strange thing happens. The beggar seems to fade away, and in his stead Launfal sees the shape of Jesus.

Jesus said, "As you did it to one of the least of these my brethren, you did it to me."

With all this talk about masks, you are probably wondering about Jesus. Is he a mask too? Hardly. He said, "He who has seen me has seen the Father."

God took off his mask when he sent Jesus. John calls Jesus "the Word made flesh." For 33 years people saw Jesus, touched him, heard him. And they loved him. He had enemies who couldn't bear his kind of love, and they crucified him. But for one moment in human history there was a divine Camelot.

But even in Jesus the world saw only a mask. After all, he looked like any other man. He was born, he grew, he played, he worked, he had friends and enemies, he died. But he rose again! He was, and is, God the Son.

Through reading about him (especially in the Gospels) and through the Holy Spirit's work in our hearts, we can learn to love him. He meets the deepest longings and yearnings of the human heart. A Hindu, hearing about him for the first time, said, "I knew God had to be like that."

Can we love him? Not with our whole heart and soul and mind (for we are sinful and selfish), but we *can* love him, and we can grow in our love of him.

God has plans

Ever since I was little I've always prayed, and I've always had a good feeling as I prayed. I felt rested, comforted. But lately I've had an uneasy feeling. Is it enough just to rest back into God? What does God do with me? Does he just let me rest in him?

Yes, he lets you rest.

You can nestle without fear. He has said that no one will be able to pluck you out of his hand. You are his forever—unless you yourself decide to leave.

But you aren't the only person in those arms. He has a place for his whole family there, and he has invited them all.

If you are counting on a quiet life with God, you and God without any interruptions, you'll soon discover that God has other plans. It's as if a young woman invites you to her apartment for dinner. You come, thinking what a good time you'll have, just the two of you, only to find that she has invited other people you don't even know. You feel that you've been tricked.

We had better be warned. God has a motley family, and they have all been invited to the party.

Or, to use another picture, you invite God into your life for some minor repairs, to ease your pain or get you a job or help you through your exams. God is the carpenter you ask to fix your leaky roof. But next thing you know, he's knocking down walls, designing new rooms, rearing up turrets — remaking the whole house. He says, "This shack isn't good enough for you. You are cramped with fear and loneliness and envy and self-pity. I want you to have a big house with rooms of joy and peace and courage. This house isn't worth patching. I'm building you a palace."

You protest, "This old house is good enough for me."

"But I'm planning to move in with you, and it isn't good enough for me. Besides, you and I can't live here alone. There are all sorts of people, your brothers and sisters, who are out in the cold crying for something better. We would never be happy, neither you nor I, if we let them wander in misery on the outside."

So his household gets bigger and bigger. And you get in deeper and deeper. It all started out with just you and God. Where in the world will it end?

Over and over again, this is what God has done to people who come to him. Let me tell you about one of them.

Sir William Wilberforce (1759-1833) was 21 when he was elected to the British Parliament. Four years later Christ caught up with him, and he gave his life to God. For a time he thought of becoming a pastor, but his friend, the younger Pitt, persuaded him to stay in Parliament and fight to make the slave traffic illegal in the empire. Wilberforce had no special love for black people, but he knew that they too were children of God. God took the love Wilberforce had for him and shifted it to the slaves.

Twenty-two years later, Wilberforce had the joy of seeing England put an end to the legal sale of slaves. That night, when Parliament took action, the speaker of the evening closed his address with these words:

I am thinking tonight of two heads and two pillows. One is the head of Napoleon, tossing feverishly on a pillow on the island of Helena, after having left a trail of blood from Jena to Waterloo. One is the man who tonight will see the consummation of his life's work. If I were to choose, I would not choose the pillow of Napoleon, but I would choose the head that will rest tonight, after our vote is taken, on the pillow of Wilberforce.

God had a surprise for Wilberforce. He brought the slaves to the party.

God has surprised millions of people. Their lives have been vastly enriched because they let God take them out of the shack, and they had all sorts of people, strangers and friends, black and white, funny people and beautiful people, join them in the palace.

This doesn't mean that you and God cannot have your private times together. You do that in your prayers and in church when you worship. But even in those moments you know you are a part of a great company. You are in a fellowship of those who, like you, have begun this life in the palace. You are also one with those on the outside who do not yet know how wonderful it is to live with God, and with all those who cry out in their loneliness and need. They are all your brothers and sisters, and your heavenly Father has maneuvered you into claiming them.

As long as you live, you'll be glad God surprised you!

Hope for peace

What scares me most about the future is nuclear power. A colonel in the Air Force told us that they talk quietly about the possibility of a two-hour war. In two hours we could all be dead. Why do we keep piling up bombs and missiles if it only means suicide for the world? Sometimes I think if that's the way it's going to be, why bother with anything?

It scares me too. But we can't give up. There may be a better day dawning. The presence of nuclear bombs and missiles may be the very thing that will at long last force nations to settle differences short of war.

War has always been madness, and nuclear war would be the final madness, the certain end of civilization. Those who survive will be back to the hoe.

No nation wants war. No mother wants her son killed. No city wants to be a pile of rubble. At the *Kirchentag,* a great gathering in Leipzig in 1954, 600,000 people heard the speaker say:

All the world longs for peace. This longing is the one common bond which, nowadays, unites torn mankind. An entirely elementary, almost banal, will demands the floor: the will to live, the thirst for existence.

People today say: we want to live, quite simply, live. We want to work. "Where we sowed the seedlings green, the golden grain we want to glean." We do not want to die. We do not want to let our children bleed to death ever again on the world's battlefields in a meaningless cause. We do not build our houses to be buried by their ruins. Our little bit of happiness, the wretched remains of our culture, our poor fragment of humanity shall not be shattered yet again.

A whole generation has been born since that day, and changes have come. We had Vietnam, but after that war the fine young men who returned hardly dared wear their uniforms. The enchantment with war had turned to cynicism. No one seemed to want war heroes.

War is peculiar business. Who were our enemies in World War II? Germany and Japan. Who was our friend? Russia. Less than a year later, Russia was the enemy and Germany and Japan our friends. We gave them billions of dollars to rebuild the cities we destroyed.

Of course, war is but the eruption into violence of problems and issues—injustice, hunger, poverty. Behind these issues lie human greed and envy.

But as never before in world history these issues have surfaced as universal concerns for all people and all nations. The United Nations' celebrated statement on human rights is more than a scrap of paper. It is the goal and the conscience for the world.

Leaders in government will tell you that issues that earlier might have threatened war are now more often settled by negotiations and treaties. A consensus of international law is emerging. The hard fact is that no great nation can afford to commit suicide by a nuclear war.

Human nature being as it is, there will always be violence that must be repelled by force. We do that within America with a police force. Some day nations may find a way to have a cooperative, international police force to do that for all the nations of the world.

We don't have to run along in the old rut. There need be no two-hour war. People have always been able to do something new, for the first time.

You and your friends who, with your guitars, have urged us "to dream the impossible dream," are called on to lead the way, to take a long stride toward the hope of peace.

You can help this old world realize the dream of Isaiah: "They shall beat their swords into plowshares, and their spears into pruning hooks; nation shall not lift up sword against nation, neither shall they learn war any more."

nothing to happen. Even so, we must always remember that we do not manipulate God, nor do our prayers prod a reluctant or sleepy God into action.

Another thing to remember is that we may by our own disobedience prevent God from doing things for us. If we pray for health and break all the rules of health, we block God out from helping. Or if we pray for a safe trip and someone else disobeys God, gets drunk, and smashes up our car, God is thwarted. If we pray for world peace and if greed and hatred plunge us into war, God can't be accused of not listening.

But keep praying. The Lord tells you to. Expect to be heard.

Perhaps we can say that there are three kinds of prayers: the give-me prayer, the make-me prayer, and the thank-you prayer. The prodigal son first asked his father, *Give me* that share of the estate that would come to me. In returning home, he prepared to ask his father, *Make me* as one of your servants. And later, he no doubt often said a *Thank-you* prayer.

Of the three, the thank-you prayer is the finest. Whatever life dishes out for you, you have countless reasons to thank God.

One of the greatest privileges is to pray for others. We are to love others as the Lord has loved us. We reach out to love and help them. Some are far away. We don't know the needs of all. But we can put them all in God's hands, in prayer.

You may not figure out everything about prayer. But pray!

God is patient

"It's remarkable how little I miss going to church. I wonder why? Once again I'm having weeks when I don't read the Bible much; I never know quite what to do about it. I have no feelings of obligation about it. . . . Of course, there's always the danger of laziness, but it would be wrong to be anxious about it. We can depend upon it that after the compass has wobbled a bit, it will point in the right direction again" (Letters and Paper from Prison, *p.* 234).

That was written by Dietrich Bonhoeffer, a great modern Christian who was imprisoned and killed by the Nazis at the age of 40. His books, *Life Together* and *Letters and Papers from Prison,* are deeply moving accounts of his life of prayer and of his faithful discipleship in the face of death. Why would a devoted Christian go through a stretch when he didn't go to church and didn't read the Bible? And why does he say that he felt no duty or obligation to do it?

Bonhoeffer speculates that he may have had a spell of being just plain lazy. But he goes on to say that he isn't worried, that though the compass wobbled a bit, it would soon point in the right direction (loving church services and the Bible).

We all have periods like that. But if laxness becomes a continuing life habit, it may mean that we're drifting away from God altogether.

As disciples of Jesus, we will have our good times and our bad times. If we hit a dull stretch of road where nothing about God excites us much, maybe that's normal. There will also be stretches where we think of Christ's love often, we pray often, and we love to be in church and sing hymns.

Another great man of God with ups and downs as a disciple was Dag Hammarskjöld of Sweden, secretary general of the United Nations. He was killed in his fifties in an airplane crash in Zambia enroute to try to end war in the Congo.

Hammarskjöld grew up in the church of Sweden, drifted from his faith at the university, and after a long search returned to the Christ of his childhood. Highly intellectual and critical and of high moral character, he describes his return to God in language that is unlike the familiar testimony:

I don't know who—or what—put the question. I don't know when it was put. I don't even remember answering. But at some moment I did answer *Yes* to Someone—or Something—and from that hour I was certain that existence is meaningful and that therefore my life of self-surrender had a goal (*Markings,* p. 169).

Faith is a gift from God. For most of us it will sometimes seem strong, sometimes weak. God deals tenderly with our weak times. In Isaiah 42:3 he says, " . . . a bruised reed he will not break, and a dimly burning wick he will not quench."

He does not reject us when our souls wander in the desert, away from the flowing waters and the soaring mountains. He waits. He knows there will be rich moments again.

He only asks that you keep going. You may feel that you find no inspiration in church, but go anyway. You don't feel like praying, but pray anyway. If you can't find words of your own, borrow from the Psalms or some book of prayers. He has promised, "Ask, and it will be given you; . . . he who seeks finds, and to him who knocks it will be opened."

God knows the road you travel. Count on him to open long vistas of joy and beauty.

Still his child

People say that God accepts me just as I am. But then someone comes along and tells me I'm not a Christian unless I shape up or unless I've had a new birth or unless I've had another baptism. I wonder if God is waiting around for me to do something before he will claim me.

Are your parents waiting for you to do something before they will claim you as their child? They may be waiting for you to shape up, but not so you might be their child. You *are* their child.

It's like that with God too. He created you to be his child, and Christ redeemed you to be his child. You don't do something to become God's child, any more than you did something to be born of your mother.

That doesn't mean you do nothing. You do a lot of things (or ought to do a lot of things) precisely *because* you are God's child.

And because you are God's child, there are some things you do not do (or ought not to do), because it is possible for you to leave God and be lost to him. But even then, you are still a child, a *lost* child, of God. And the Bible says that you could be lost to him forever.

89

How far can you go before you are lost to him? No one can say. Only God knows. But if you are worried about having drifted away from him, God isn't as concerned as he would be if you never bothered to worry.

God wants you to think of what he has done to make you his child and to keep you his child. He doesn't want you to fret over what you can do or feel or experience so you can be his child. If you examine yourself instead of looking at Christ, you'll be asking one or more of the following questions:

- Do I feel enough to be a Christian?
- Do I do enough to be a Christian?
- Do I have the right experiences to be a Christian?
- Do I have the right doctrines to be a Christian?

You'll never be able to answer these questions well enough to be sure that you are a Christian.

You are a Christian because Christ died on a cross to take away your sins and to give you the right to be with the Father. You count on him—not on yourself. You must not torment yourself with endless self-questioning. You can rest back into Christ and his love for you.

This doesn't mean that you are satisfied with yourself or that God is satisfied with you. Many things about you he would like to see different. After all, you are his child, and the hopes and expectations he has for his children are high. He would like you to be like him.

The Holy Spirit is present to help you become more and more Christ-like. He has a chance to shape you into the Jesus-image if you hear his Word and come to his Supper, if you try to help anyone in need and pray to him and thank him.

Don't worry about how you might feel; he will give you the feelings he wants you to have. Simply *do* those things that will give him a chance to do something for you.

If you live to be 90, God will want to use the years to usher you further and further into the riches of his kingdom. He doesn't want to leave you on the far borders or let you slip away altogether. You are his child, and he is eager to have you live like his child.

How could he want less for you?

Future hopes

Tell me, what does your generation really think of my graduating class? Are we worse, better, or about the same as high school kids when you finished school? If you think we're worse, you're usually careful not to say so. If we're better, you hardly dare admit it. And how about yourselves—has your generation grown wiser and better through the years?

I can tell you what *I* think. That may or may not be the consensus of other older adults.

You experiment more than we did. When our parents told us, "Don't swim too close to that place in the river—it has a hidden whirlpool," we would likely take their word. You want to find out for yourselves. Some of you get sucked in and destroyed. Most of you get out in time. When your turn comes to be parents you will hope that your children will believe you and be spared the dangers and hurts.

You may not be more honest, but you're more candid, more open. Of course, the rest of the world has become more open too. For instance, the restraints and mystery have been stripped from sex. You have been robbed of the enchantment of the hidden and mysterious.

You are heirs to rapid change and victims of greater insecurity. You are not as sure as we were that the world is a safe place. You are tempted, therefore, to question the time-tested values of hard work, fair play, patriotism, and personal integrity.

Even so, I believe you are a more serious generation than the graduates 25 years ago. For a while, older people thought that beards, long hair, patched jeans, and bare feet were signs that young people had given up on everything stable and good. Now we know that's not true.

In fact, we have the uneasy feeling that with your nonconformity you are telling us something we need to hear—for instance, that success is not to be measured by big homes and cars and bank accounts. I am much encouraged by many of your age group who look forward to doing something in life that will help other people.

In my youth I lived in a sheltered world. My father had a general store in the same little town for 46 years. Most people there had the same ideas about right and wrong. But your generation rubs shoulders with people who have many different ideas of what's good and what isn't good. You have to find your way.

What you will discover, I think, is that most of the values your parents and grandparents cherish are the ones you gradually will return to as your own. Some of their values may not be worth keeping. If so, I hope you will discard them for better ones. But don't be in a hurry about that. What you think may be a phony bit of polished glass may really be a diamond.

There are stirrings in the religious life of your generation that would have been harder to find a few decades ago. You are not afraid to confess openly your commitment to Jesus Christ, to wear a cross, and to tell others that you go to church and that you pray.

Through TV, reading, and travel, you have more awareness that this is one world, and that we will have to seek peace and the common welfare together. I hope you will love your country not only as a great nation, but also as a contributor to the world's good.

Our hopes for the future are in you, after all. We are often painfully aware that we are not turning over to you an easy job or an untroubled world. It's almost as if a man turns over his farm to his son, only to have the son learn that it has both a first and a second mortgage. But we have to count on you. And we do.

When I was 12, my father took me with him on the train. The porter asked me, "Are you going to be as good a man as your father?" I'll never forget my father's quick retort: "He's going to be a better man than his father." Every generation hopes and believes that of the next generation. Will you rise to meet the challenge?

Why do I pray?

Yes, I pray, but I'm not sure why. How can I make God change his mind, or remind him of my needs, if he already loves me and knows what I need? It's hard to think that God would hold up some blessings just because I didn't ask for them.

You don't talk to your parents only when you want something. Most likely your best times with them are just good talk when you don't ask for anything. They love you and of course are concerned with your needs and wants, but most of all they want you, and want you to want them.

God wants you, and wants you to want him. Whatever else you may want or need, the greatest gift God can give you is himself.

Occasionally I've wondered if the Lord urges us to pray for anything and everything primarily to get us to keep talking to him, and not because he wants to be reminded of what we need. He knows our needs without our prayers, but if we didn't talk with him, he would be lonely.

We can't dismiss prayer with such a simple explanation, however. There is mystery in the ways of God. Prayer does change things—and people.

There are many instances of prayer releasing healing and strength. Nor would the Lord tell us again and again to call on him if he expected

83